CRAFT FAIL

When Homemade
Goes Horribly Wrong

HEATHER MANN

Founder and chief executive failer at CraftFail.com

Workman Publishing
New York

Library of Congress Cataloging-in-Publication Data is available.
ISBN 978-0-7611-7992-4

Design by Becky Terhune
Front cover image by Monica McCready
Back cover image by Summer Donily
Design elements: Fail stamp, Balint Radu/Fotolia; gold frames, Zakharov Evgeniy/Fotolia; thumbs-down icon, atScene/Fotolia.

Additional image credits on pages 161–167. All other images courtesy of the author.

Workman books are available at special discounts when purchased in bulk for premiums and sales promotions as well as for fund-raising or educational use. Special editions or book excerpts also can be created to specification. For details, contact the Special Sales Director at the address below, or send an email to specialmarkets@workman.com.

Workman Publishing Company, Inc.
225 Varick Street
New York, NY 10014-4381
workman.com

WORKMAN is a registered trademark of Workman Publishing Co., Inc.

Printed in the United States of America
First printing September 2014

10 9 8 7 6 5 4 3 2 1

Contents

Introduction: The Worst Failer in the World 1

Take the Quiz: Are You an All-Star CraftFailer? 4

Chapter 1: Home Decor Fails 7

Chapter 2: Fashion Fails 23

Chapter 3: Holiday Fails 41

Chapter 4: Food Fails 67

Chapter 5: Martha Made It 105

Chapter 6: Kids. Crafts. Fails. 117

Chapter 7: A for Effort 135

Contributors and Credits 161

Acknowledgments 168

About the Author 169

Introduction
The Worst Failer in the World

When I was a kid, things came easily to me. I didn't put much effort into anything. I got straight As, was a naturally talented singer, and had an aptitude for art. I also had little patience: If I wasn't good at something on the first or second try, I would get frustrated and quit because "I didn't want to do it anyway." This do-it-well-or-quit-before-anyone-sees-me-try mentality lasted throughout my teens and even into my twenties, when I finally maxed out all the things I could naturally do well on the first try, and I actually had to apply myself.

Throughout my early life, I kept a list of things I was good at and made sure to stay away from things I wasn't so hot at. Journalism and musical theater, in. Volleyball and snowboarding, OUT. The frustration I experienced during the failures was so crippling that I never allowed myself to work hard to improve. I have always been ashamed of this early lack of character.

As I got older and learned to manage my frustration a little better, I discovered a few areas that I enjoyed despite not having any particular aptitude for them. Because these were things that were not on my "I'm so good at this" list, I let myself completely off the perfection hook. I liked sewing, but somehow my beginner's dress came out with a wrong-facing fabric bodice or a hooded coat had a small, constricting neck. Because I didn't count sewing among my "talents," I didn't beat myself up about failing; I just let the handmade garment stay in the back of my closet, or left it unfinished and moved on.

One of my earliest "craftfail" memories was when I was seven and my mom was making hand-drawn paper dolls with me and my sister, Shannon. I could *not* understand why my mom's paper dolls were drawn so well and mine looked like a seven-year-old child had made them. So disproportionate, such wobbly lines. Hers looked like real princesses and mine looked like mutant princesses from the planet Gorsnatch.

"I've had years of practice, Heather," my mom told me. "You can't compare your seven-year-old's drawings to an adult's." Grudgingly, I admitted to myself that she had a point. It didn't make my princesses look better, but I could see that there was a sliding scale of skill level, of which I would have had to start at one end and work my way up.

Unrealistic expectations are one of the major contributing factors to a typical craftfail. A novice baker expects her three-tiered rainbow splatter cake to look exactly like *Ace of Cakes*' Duff Goldman's, but Duff has made 14,372 cakes, and this beginner has made only a few in her entire life. I am willing to bet Duff's first three-tiered cake was lumpy and misshapen, too.

Enough about Duff—back to me. As a professional craft blogger and general craft enthusiast, I regularly go where no crafter has gone before (or, at least, I like to try out new skills), and most crafts have a learning curve that can't be avoided. Because I have to learn to use new materials and tinker around with new techniques, I have created hundreds of unappealing prototypes. Before CraftFail.com, I would chuck them, so no one could see my mistakes and realize I wasn't the Mozart of crafting.

The day after I started the CraftFail blog, however, an interesting thing happened. Readers responded right away because they identified with the crushed expectations of a Jabba the Hutt–sized knitted beanie or a dog poop–like frosting fail. I began to look forward to failing, and my readers enjoyed laughing at me. Because of CraftFail.com, so many people have told me "now I don't feel so alone in my failure!"

Throughout the years, I have posted craftfails of my own and those shared by other crafters, and I've become a full-on failure enthusiast. I finally learned what never got through to me as a failure-phobic kid: We learn a heck of a lot more by failing than we ever will by succeeding on the first try.

CraftFail is a celebration of the creative process, but unlike those perfect magazine shots and idealized online inspiration boards, we showcase the gruesome underbelly of the creative process—the "try, try again," the "A for effort," that special moment when you take a step back . . . and hope nobody else is looking. With *CraftFail,* I seek to celebrate the learning process and the nature of creativity. I do not want anyone to be discouraged from trying, but instead to be encouraged by the society of creative failers who are brave enough to share their craft blunders.

In my eyes, craftfails are beautiful because they are tangible evidence of the learning process. I value my ability to fail—it's the most important thing I've taken thirty years to learn.

TAKE THE QUIZ!

1. When you began your craft, you:
- **A.** Didn't read instructions.
- **B.** Misread instructions.
- **C.** Ignored instructions.
- **D.** Knew better than instructions.

2. When getting your project materials together, you:
- **A.** Substituted key materials.
- **B.** Substituted one too many materials.
- **C.** Substituted every material in the project.
- **D.** Substituted alcohol consumption for material gathering.

3. While preparing your project components, you:
- **A.** Measured wrong.
- **B.** Measured right and cut wrong.
- **C.** Measured right and attached wrong.
- **D.** What is this *measuring* of which you speak?

Star CraftFailer?

4. While assembling your craft, you:
  A. Cut corners.
  B. Cut corners off.
  C. Cut wrong pattern pieces.
  D. Cut it out of ugly fabric.

5. When you dreamed of your project before you began, you:
  A. Imagined being happy at the end of the project.
  B. Imagined giving the project to a happy gift recipient.
  C. Imagined making hundreds of them to sell to happy buyers on Etsy and at local craft markets.
  D. Imagined Martha Stewart happily offering you a million dollars for your amazing craft idea.

6. The project level of the craft you undertook was:
  A. Right for my experience level.
  B. Challenging yet possible for my experience level.
  C. Probably reaching a bit for my experience level.
  D. Experience? I don't need no stinkin' experience.

7. When checking the lettering on your project, you:

    A. Forgot to proofread.

    B. Forgot to flip letters in the right direction.

    C. Forgot that you can't spell.

    D. Forgot that there aren't four Ms in Mommmy.

8. At the conclusion of the project, you swear it wasn't you because—crappy directions, see?

    A. The directions didn't take into account that my oven's temperature runs hot.

    B. The directions didn't take into account that I read only the first sentence of every paragraph. It's a speed-reading technique I learned in college.

    C. The directions didn't tell me to avoid using clashing fabrics.

    D. The directions didn't mention that the inspiration photo was completely Photoshopped.

Scoring: Let's just assume you're a craftfailer and move on.

Chapter 1

HOME DECOR FAILS

Home is where the heart is, and handmade home decor from the heart helps make a house a home. When you put your personal touch on a piece of wall art or a throw pillow, it adds a bit of coziness to the place where you spend your days and nights. It may also add a touch of unwanted tackiness to the landscape.

Home decor objects are meant to stay at home, after all, so, when you fail, there's no escaping that unfortunate melted crayon art project or droopy plaster taxidermy head hanging over the mantle. Don't worry, though; we'll be there to hold you while you cry . . . so long as you let us share your living room fail with the world.

Be Still My Heart-Shaped Wreath

Iuliana pinned a sweet Valentine's Day project to her inspiration board—a burlap wreath fashioned over a wire coat hanger.

After a struggle to create the wreath, she quit trying to coax the stubborn hanger into a heart shape and got all Joan Crawford on that craft's ass. No more burlap-covered wire hangers. Ever.

Papier Mâché Animal Bust

When the trend of decorating with faux animal busts was on the rise, Meg spent a whole day creating the most beautiful stag from papier mâché.

As soon as she mounted the animal bust to the wall and proudly documented her success via all available social media channels, her creation went from success to failure.

BUSTED PAPIER MÂCHÉ ANIMAL

FAIL

There it hangs, her first-ever documented craftfail: caught, stuffed, and mounted.

Insanely Easy No-Sew Pillow Cover

Melissa found a simple pillow cover tutorial on the blog OrganizeYourStuffNow.com and decided she would reclaim some "nasty, kidified pillows" using the clever folding and knotting technique. Simply fold the fabric around the pillow, tie, and you're done!

INSANITY-INSPIRED PILLOW COVER

FAIL

I call it "straitjacket chic."

Chevron Stained Glass

Michelle's Theory:
Tinted Mod Podge, when stenciled onto glass, will allow light to shine through and create a stained-glass-window effect.

FAIL

Michelle's Conclusion:
Tinted Mod Podge, when peeled from the stencil, may be placed into a pile, creating a broken stained-glass-window effect.

Gina
I like reading about other people's fails . . . makes mine seem okay.

The Beautiful Button Bowl

It starts with an intriguing concept: Create a bowl out of buttons and glue using a balloon as a base! Like papier mâché. But with buttons. And no paper.

POPPED A BUTTON BOWL

Juliet's dreams deflated shortly after the balloon wheezed its last bit of air.

BLOWN BUTTON BOWL

Madison blew her chances of a button bowl when the balloon imploded.

PENNY DREADFUL FAIL

Christine tried to make the button bowl with pennies. That's 87 cents she's never getting back.

Darling 3-Dimensional Wall Art

Emily was inspired by a simple-yet-elegant wall art project she found on Pinterest. Simply decorate a canvas with glue, puff paint–style, and finish it off with a layer of spray paint. So, she used puff paint on a coloring book page and covered it with sheer silver paint.

OH, DEER, 3-DIMENSIONAL ART?

A stag-gering work of heartbreaking genius.

Melted Crayon Canvas Rainbow

The melted crayon canvas is one of the most pinned and repinned projects on Pinterest. The concept? Attach crayons to a blank canvas, then melt the crayons with a hairdryer to create colorful, one-of-a-kind melted-wax wall art.

FAIL

(where there's smoke . . .)

Courtney got too close with the heat source and the whole canvas went up in flames. Like I said, this project is SUPER HOT on Pinterest.

Paint Chip Collage

Crafter Alyssa saw this cute paint chip collage and knew she could pull off this colorful art project: All she had to do was glue pieces of paper to a board. *Kindergartners do this on a regular basis,* she thought. But Alyssa used a restickable glue stick instead of the regular kind.

PAINT CHIP FAIL-AGE

The verdict: Chips started shifting and falling off immediately, revealing a deep gash in the surface of the backing board. The moral: Substitutions for key materials can lead to colossal craftfail.

Paisley Patio Umbrella

Michelle added a stamped and stenciled paisley design in an attempt to rejuvenate her faded patio umbrella. She was happy because it turned out just as pretty as she had envisioned.

PAISLEY POO-BRELLA

FAIL

Then she sat down at the table and looked up. The antique white paint, combined with the irregular bloblike stencil pattern color, made the umbrella look like it had been crapped on by a flock of large and extremely incontinent birds.

Talented birds, though—birds that poop paisley.

Song of the Stiff String Spheres

Stiffy, a useful product with an amusing name, is used to stiffen fabric and yarn. But crafters the world over employ it to achieve a classic, understated table centerpiece: The Decorative String Sphere. Simply inflate a balloon and wrap Stiffy-soaked string or yarn around it. Let the string dry, and pop the balloon; the yarn should preserve the shape of the balloon! So many crafters tried, while so many crafters failed. . . .

GRAVITY BALLS

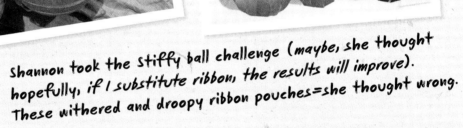

Shannon took the stiffy ball challenge (maybe, she thought hopefully, if I substitute ribbon, the results will improve). These withered and droopy ribbon pouches=she thought wrong.

IF THESE BALLS COULD TALK

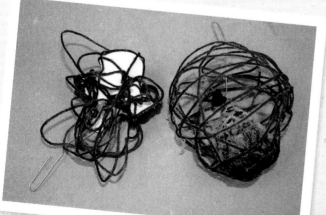

When Amy's balloon was popped, a gross, crusty mess flaked everywhere. One of the yarn balls threw itself off the drying rack in despair.

GREAT BALLS OF FAILURE

BOTCHED BALLOON ANIMAL BALLS

Carla got creative with her balloon selection: "I went with long, twisty balloons, like you'd use to make balloon animals." She subdivided the balloons into smaller, rounder segments for wrapping. Her theory seemed promising . . .

Maybe the project works better when scaled up: Amanda wound string around a beach ball, while visions of a beautiful modern light fixture danced in her head.

CRY ME A GLITTER

Even Glitter Mod Podge can't save this project.

NO REST FOR THE SHRIVELED

Haley's balloon didn't even make it out of the ball.

TRY, TRY AGAIN

Tracy made many sad attempts. We'll just count them as one big FAIL.

Plaster Mask Planter Task

Jenn was inspired by one of crafting guru Mark Montano's outdoor projects: a planter adorned with a plaster cast mask. Say that five times fast.

PLASTER MASK PLANTER MUSH

Instead of reading the directions, she added the plaster in a freeform style. Her technique resulted in a planter that resembles the love child of Cookie Monster and cement mixer.

Chapter 2
FASHION FAILS

Do-it-yourself fashion is as popular as ever, with inspirational tutorials in fashion mags and on blogs helping you deck yourself out from head to toe. We don't want to be left out of the fashion week party, so we've dedicated a chapter to sharing with you what's hot—well, more like what's not—in DIY fashion. Here are some tips: T-shirts aren't as easy to cut up as you think, Boho chic can quickly go Sister wife–esque, and elaborate nail art takes practice. Still want to try to customize your own personal style with some DIY projects? Good news: We've got you covered with ginormous hats, ink-stained shirts, and botched glitter shoes.

The 20-Minute T-Shirt Dress

The project was so simple and so inspirational: Attach a tank top or T-shirt to a couple yards of fabric, and in 20 minutes, you have yourself a cute little summer dress! $20 and four hours later . . .

DIY SISTER WIFE T-SHIRT DRESS

FAIL

Sister wives? Sister, why would you ever wear that?

Fashion with Scissors

Inspired by this woven jersey (that's Pinterest for "T-shirt fabric") shirt project, Tess optimistically substituted ribbon for the fabric strips and enthusiastically attacked her tank top.

FAIL

Edward Scissorhands called. He wants his tank top back.

These Are Spray-Painted Shoes

Jessica wanted pink neon heels (doesn't everybody?). Pinterest told her she could spray paint some boring brown heels she found in the back of her closet. She even read all of the instructions (down to coating the shoes in primer before hitting them with the pink paint). They turned out *exactly* like she imagined!

THESE ARE SPRAY-PAINTED SHOES ON CRACK

FAIL

Then she walked in them. No one ever pins a picture of the spray-painted shoes after they've been worn.

Woven Scarf Wars

Crafterella asks: How exactly does one fail at making a scarf? It's just a long, skinny rectangle! After hours and hours of weaving, she knew it had gone horribly wrong, but she was too stubborn to quit.

AMISH-DALA'S HEADSCARF STRIKES BACK

FAIL

Coming very soon, to a blog near you: the pattern for a crazy Amish Amidala (cough, Star Wars, cough) headscarf, along with some steamy Pennsylvania Dutch/Star Wars mash-up fan fiction.

Downton Abbey DO: Doily Necklace

Inspired by the maids' attire from her favorite show, *Downton Abbey,* Shannon designed a lace doily necklace.

DOWNTON ABBEY DON'T: STARCH NECKLACE

(does not bend) ↗

FAIL

There's nothing wrong with lace and ruffles, Shannon. But maybe lay off the starch.

Union Jack Knit Cap ✳

Experience won't exempt anyone from entering the CraftFail Hall of Fame. Just ask Kelly, a talented knitter, who decided to make this *tuque* (that's Canadian for "knit cap") for her British son-in-law. Six balls of yarn . . . for a hat? She didn't hear the crafty police sirens that were obviously blaring. When she finished felting the hat (shrink to fit!), it came out looking like a giant tea cozy.

UNION JACK CRANIUM COZY

FAIL

Kelly offered to cut two holes and add suspenders to make it into a pair of Canuck swimming trunks instead.

Madison
Haha, looks like England is doomed.

HOW DO YOU SPELL MOMMMY?

jaycee's
mommmy

Brandy created a custom tank top for her cousin, who loved it, and wore it a few times before her husband spotted the extra M that no one had ever noticed.

Stacy O.
Too funny! I picture it being said with a whine . . . Moooommmmyy!

Sharon C.
You could think of it this way: She puts the mmm into Mommmy!

THE GREAT FRANKENSTEIN WESTWOOD MISCALCULATION

Carmen used Butterick pattern 9214 to make a coat dress— with just a few modifications. To be fair, she nicknamed it the Frankenpattern because of all the bits and pieces she added to the garment to turn it into the dress of her dreams. (Read: she made it more difficult.)

She sewed it in a pretty tartan plaid, inspired by a Vivienne Westwood gown, and after seeing a hooded Derek Lam design, she decided her garment needed a shawl collar hood as well. It's alive! And not in a good way.

FAIL

SCARFING SOME BACON

FAIL

Long, skinny scarves were all the rage, and Amanda was so excited to create her own cute little accessory. Then she put it on.

That's when it became clear: BACON SCARF!!!

Everything's better with bacon... right?

GINORMOUS SHOWER CAP

FAIL

For Bridgit's first attempt at making a frilly shower cap, she overestimated the size of her head.

Good for protecting your makeup in the shower?

Ink Stain Shirt

Carla found an impressive-looking ink stain shirt tutorial online. Just your basic artful staining of a shirt using droplets of ink—then wash in cold water to set the color. Here's what Carla ended up with:

A pink shirt . . .

. . . and a pink towel.

Julie
We just coined a term at our blog. *Pintrick:* when someone posts something on Pinterest and they make it look simple, but when you try to do it the whole thing is a disaster. Usage: "I was Pintricked!"

Glinda's Glitter Shoes

Lindsey thought it looked easy to make glitter shoes. Just click your heels together three times . . .

. . . to create an icky, goopy mess.

FAIL

Marbled Nail Art

EPIC FAIL

Before Pinterest, we didn't even know nail art was a thing. The water-marbled manicure makes for impressively colorful and intricate fingernails, and the instructions seem deceptively simple: Drip nail polish on water, swirl it, dip your nails under the water, and you have yourself an amazing technicolor dream manicure. After receiving dozens of photos from marbled nail failers, we deemed the water-marbled manicure an Epic Fail.

MARBLE MAY I

Thinking I could pull this manicure off? I must have lost my marbles.

CAPTURE THE BAG

Gina: "I so badly wanted to have pretty, swirly, marbled nails, but when I tried dropping my second color of polish on top of the water, it looked like a blood clot on top of a wet plastic sack."

DRIP TEASE

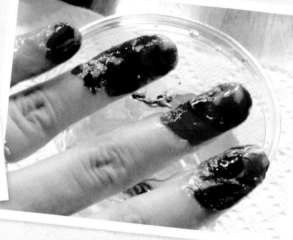

Sonja: "Who would do this to themselves on purpose?"

NAILS FROM THE CRYPT

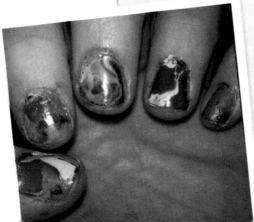

Stephanie: "My nails look like something from the zombie Apocalypse."

Shoot her! Shoot her!

The Magic Marble Manicure

IT CAN BE DONE

The inspiration photos for marbled nails are so enticing that even I, a veteran craftfailer, just had to try it for myself. In 10 messy minutes, I lubed up my nails with petroleum jelly to make cleanup easier. (I hoped the Vaseline would offer some pleasant side effects and soothe my ragged cuticles.) I dripped the polish into the water. I submerged my whole hand into the tiny cup like a family of clowns in a Smartcar. I pulled my nails out for the reveal, and . . . there was nail polish all over my whole hand.

I quickly dripped polish into the cup again and dipped my other hand. The existing scum on the top of the water married hideously with the new polish, which made an awful, ugly, blumpy mess on my left hand. And the Vaseline didn't really help with cleanup or my cuticles.

Turns out, it's very difficult to get water-marbled nails right on the first try, and it is a long and laborious process. You can't cut any corners, and there is no way to predict the final outcome of your nails. Even the pros sometimes get bubbles or an ugly swirl or an unpredictable color result.

Continued →

Tips, in case you still decide to do water-marbled nails:

1. You must do a basecoat, preferably two. For best results, use a light color such as white or nude.

2. Cover your cuticle to help speed up the cleanup. Successful marble manicurists cut pieces of tape that fit around your finger and trim away the section where your nail is.

3. You must work quickly because the nail polish begins to dry out as it spreads on the water.

4. Marble only one nail at a time.

5. You must keep your nail submerged underwater while you skim the surface of the water for all the excess nail polish. Only when the surface is clean can you bring your nail up out of the water.

6. Put a clear topcoat on your nails after the marbled finish is dry to protect the design for a few days.

Follow these tips, and you will meet with at least slight success. The process will still take you about an hour from start to finish, but your nails will be fabulous. And sometimes, it's worth following instructions in the name of style.

Chapter 3
HOLIDAY FAILS

The holidays have a kind of magic: a magic that lures you into thinking you'll be able to make perfectly decorated gingerbread men (with your angelic preschoolers, who won't get a bit of frosting on the counter), give a gorgeous handmade gift to everyone in the tri-county area, and put on an elegant dinner that will even impress your mother-in-law.

I do believe in the magic of a handmade holiday, but I don't believe that handmade makes a holiday perfect. Handmade can make a holiday stressful, distract you from your family because you're staying up late to hot glue your gifts together, or lead to disappointment on the faces of gift recipients who would rather receive "real soap" from Bath & Body Works.

To me, the true magic of the holidays is that people believe they can craft something. They might not believe it the rest of the year, but at Christmas, they're right there in Santa's workshop, whipping up magical creations with the rest of the elves.

Kitschy Holiday Toilet Seat Cover

Growing up in the '80s, Lindsay had a toilet seat cover with Santa on the top, and when you lifted the lid you saw him again, covering his eyes. Since this awesome relic was lost to the ages, she decided to re-create it for her own home. She proudly decked the toilet with the Snowman toilet seat cover and showed her husband.

POLAR PLUNGE

FAIL

While the top was great, when he lifted the lid, it was a 180-degree fail—and Lindsay just had to share it since it was "too crappy" to keep to herself.

Toilet Paper Tube Wreath

Some people can spin cardboard into crafty gold. Or at least, spiral toilet paper tubes into a pretty holiday wreath.

FAIL

And then there's the rest of us. We cut toilet paper tubes and they just look like cut-up toilet paper tubes.

Innocent Easter Bunny and Carrot Craft

Professional craft designer
Amanda designed a bunny
family out of cardboard tubes
for her craft blog.
The concept included little carrots
made out of orange and green
chenille stems with rabbit paws
made of little round pom-poms
on either side.
Great concept. The execution was
a little flawed, however.

FREUDIAN CARROT

Sometimes a carrot is not just a carrot.

Pretty Peppermint Wreath

Brittany made a fetching peppermint candy wreath for the holidays, and it hung on her front door for a few weeks, but North Carolina's weather had more sinister plans. The temperature rose to 70°F in December, and the muggy, wet days bedeviled Brittany's wreath.

POSSESSED PEPPERMINT WREATH

FAIL

Brittany opened her door to a pool of sticky red on the doorstep. Then she realized: This peppermint wreath was BLEEDING!

It's hard to remember the date, y'all. Just check your calendar before you get your wood-burning tool out.

Because you can't UNBURN it.

Stained-Glass-Window Cookies

'Tis the season to make cookies, fa-la-la-la-laaaa, la-la-la-FAIL! For these stained-glass delicacies, you roll out sugar cookie dough, cut a star-shaped decorative hole in each one, and fill the hole with crushed hard candy. The heat of the oven melts the candy into edible stained-glass windows.

BROKEN-GLASS-WINDOW COOKIES

FAIL

Tracy tried. Tracy fa-la-la-la-failed.

Peppermint Platter Perfection

Pinterest would have us believe that melted hard candies make great craft materials. As Kristen discovered, it's not as easy as you might think to melt peppermints into a gorgeous serving tray.

PEPPERMINT PLATTER PUDDLE

FAIL

But making a molten mound of peppermint? Totally doable.

Betty's Bunny Cake

Every year Shelly attempts a bunny cake. "This year I saw Betty Crocker's adorable bunny cake made with coconut. The kids wanted to help, but I said, 'No, no, . . . this one is for Mom to do so it turns out just right.'"

BAD BUNNY CAKE

"When my friends asked, I told them the kids had a great time decorating the cake."

Oreo Reindeer Pops

Oreo reindeer pops are a quick and easy way to make a tasty holiday treat. Hey, there's no baking involved! Well, you do have to melt chocolate, but that's about it. That leaves only one question. . . .

FAIL

How do you harden the chocolate after it's melted?

Reindeer Marshmallow Studs

No-bake reindeer pops can also be made from marshmallows! When she was shopping for supplies, Iliana forgot that reindeer have eyes. She improvised and used what she had on hand.

REINDEER MARSHMALLOW DUDS

FAIL

. . . Milk Duds, that is.

Cute Hard-Boiled Chicks

Hard-boiled eggs turned into
adorable peeping chicks?
Yes, please.

NUCLEAR CHICKEN MELTDOWN

These deviled eggs weren't as easy
as they were cracked up to be.

Intricate Easter Eggs

Madelyn got a Ukrainian Easter Egg kit as a gift and thought, *Wow, what amazing designs!* The process was a little more involved than she expected.

FAIL

After a few squiggles, Madelyn knew she'd be submitting a photo to CraftFail.

Pumpkin Glitter Greatness

Anna used Elmer's glue and glitter to create these gorgeous sparkly pumpkins, and at first they were the stars of the stoop, the pretties of the porch, the darlings of the doorstep. But then? Rain happened.

Here's a fun fact: Did you know that white glue, even after it dries, is water soluble?

PUMPKIN'S GOTTA GIVE

green beans?

Like magic, the rain separated this craft into two piles: one pile for pumpkins, and another for shiny stuff that used to be stuck to aforementioned pumpkins.

GINGERBREAD HOUSE OF HORRORS

PEPPARKAKSHUS:
Hard to say,
harder to build

we tried
I sware
we tried

FAIL

William and Demetra went out to dinner, leaving their teens to assemble the Ikea gingerbread house. This is what they came home to.

Candy Easter Bouquet

Sarah found the perfect flower arrangement, punctuated with marshmallow bunnies, to make for her mom.
She assembled it on Saturday and kept it in a closet for safekeeping overnight. When she pulled it out Easter morning, it was a big hit with her mother.

ANT-Y EASTER BOUQUET

FAIL

(so elegANT!)

Sadly, the candy bunnies were also a big hit with the six-legged anthill types.

Día de los Muertos Sugar Skull

Dianna's friend asked her to make sugar skulls for a traditional Día de los Muertos celebration.

DÍA DE LOS FAILS

¡Ay, Dios mío!

FAIL

"I should never ever be allowed to touch icing. Ever."

Turkey Cookie

Alissa was inspired by these turkey cookies she saw on the blog Lizy B. Bakes. She just knew they'd be the perfect addition to her Thanksgiving celebration.

TOTAL TURKEY

festive headdress?

FAIL

Every part of Alissa's turkey cookie turned out as sad as an actual turkey on Thanksgiving.

Turkey Cookie Cuties

Jennifer works as the activity director at a home for seniors, where she had an afternoon cooking class scheduled. Unable to find candy corn in the store, she had to improvise quickly and thought M&Ms would work just fine.

FAIL

M&Ms work great if you like your turkey cookies to look like they just got back from the hairdresser. In the 1950s.

The Rickrack Flag Shirt

When Gina found this inspiration project, she thought, *How hard can it be to arrange rickrack in straight lines on a T-shirt?*

THE RICKRACK ATTACK SHIRT

Old Glory, not looking so glorious.

Witch Finger Cookies

Shoni was invited to participate in a Halloween bake sale at work and came up with the perfect creepy treat: witch finger cookies. The severed digits were looking so great when she put them in the oven that she even did a little victory dance around the kitchen. Then she opened the oven.

SMASHED WITCH FINGER COOKIES

FAIL

"I'll get you my pretties . . . and your little cookies, too!" shouted the Wicked Witch of the West before Dorothy's house landed on her fingers.

THE RED REINDEER MASSACRE

FAIL

Kim: "God bless my elderly neighbor for giving us these reindeer cookies for Christmas. . . .

. . . Unfortunately, they came decapitated and covered in blood."

Paint Drip Pumpkin

Alexa from theswelldesigner.com is known for her awesome Halloween crafts, and her idea to mash up the paint drip trend with the faux pumpkin craft trend was no different.

PUMPKIN WICKED THIS WAY COMES

Pin this to your "toxic waste ideas" inspiration board.

Let's Bring the Holidays Down a Notch

Kristen Howerton, RageAgainstTheMinivan.com

The pressure put on today's parents to trip the light crafttastic is just unrealistic. Facebook friends post updates about elaborate birthday parties they've put together (Status update: "Up at 3 a.m. to make cupcakes for Ezra's 2nd birthday party!"). The Internet is awash with crafts and cute snacks for even the most obscure holidays. (Did you know Jelly Bean Day is April 22nd? A Pinterest board told me so.).

Today was St. Patrick's Day, a holiday we had completely forgotten about until our son stumbled into the living room at about 11:30 p.m. last night. "Can I help you guys hide the gold coins?" he asked. The WHAT? "The gold coins. I know the leprechauns aren't real. I know it's you, like Santa, so I want to help. I can make the leprechaun trap, too."

We told him to go to bed and then looked at each other with exasperation. Gold coins? A leprechaun trap? When I was a kid, we celebrated St. Patrick's Day by wearing something green. THE END. But over the past few years, our kids had been coming home from school with grander ideas.

The sun came up and the kids ran into our room, clamoring like it was Christmas morning. "Did a leprechaun visit? Can we search for him? Did he leave a pot of gold? Let's go find the gold coins!"

So. Many. Expectations. All of which were dashed. I had four seriously disappointed kids—and one with a full-blown meltdown, kicking random items in her room and yelling about what a lame holiday this was.

People. St. Patrick's Day is supposed to be a "phone-it-in" holiday. Seriously, enough with the holiday overkill. As if Christmas wasn't already hard enough as a parent, someone also decided that we have to move an elf around every day, into creative tableaus? And then someone else decided that the Advent calendar was a thing that now involves some kind of gift each day leading up to Christmas? And about a month after having survived that whole mess, Valentine's Day has become the new Halloween, for which a simple store-bought card won't suffice. You'd better include some candy or your child will be shunned. Shunned! One of my kids came home from class with a whole freaking goodie bag!

Hey, overachieving parent who started this goodie bag trend . . . I've got a message for you. It's a homemade Valentine card that my kid made. I'd originally pulled it out of the rotation, but I'd like to use it now.

I don't like the feeling of disappointing my kids. But I refuse to give in to this holiday overkill. I'm overwhelmed enough as it is. Today, I gave all of my kids a bath. We read with each of them for the recommended twenty minutes. We sat together at the table and ate a meal that wasn't procured at a drive-through. We played outside.

Fellow parents . . . teachers . . . Sunday school workers . . . I beseech you. Bring it down a notch. Give a failer a break. Y'all are setting up expectations that I just can't maintain. I can go big for Christmas and Easter, but that's all I can handle. Wouldn't we all be just a little happier if we returned to the slacker days of store-bought Valentines and kit-dyed eggs and just wearing a green shirt and calling it a day?

For the sake of overwhelmed parents everywhere, stop the madness!

Chapter 4

FOOD FAILS

Everybody eats. And anybody who cooks has botched a recipe at least once. Food fails are the most frequent submissions that cross the CraftFail desk. And we're here to share the rotten fruits of their labor.

Here are some tips for those who don't want to fail at food: Check your larder to make sure you have all the required ingredients BEFORE you start baking, be aware that chocolate isn't as easy to melt as it looks, and think twice before you try to make a rainbow-colored dessert.

So-and-so said, "If you can read, you can cook." But what happens if you don't read before you cook?

Food fails happen. The good news: You can (almost always) eat the evidence.

Rainbow Cake in a Jar

I love the smell of Rainbow Cake in a Jar in the morning!

NAPALM CAKE IN A JAR

Just beware the toxic technicolor mushroom cloud shooting from the top.

HOLE-BAKED BREAD

FAIL

Now with 40 percent fewer calories.

Melted Marshmallow Frosting

EPIC FAIL

According to a leading lifestyle magazine, you can melt marshmallows on top of your cupcakes instead of frosting. Just pop them on top of the cupcakes about three minutes before you are due to take the cupcakes out of the oven. Let the marshmallow warm up and then squash it down for instant no-fuss frosting. Marshmallows are not happy about this article. . . .

THE MELTED MARSHMALLOW MUTINY

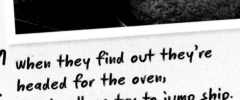

When they find out they're headed for the oven, marshmallows try to jump ship.

When they discover they're stuck in the oven, they dig down into the cupcakes, preparing for further guerrilla warfare.

After exiting the fiery furnace, they spring back resiliently, despite their war wounds, refusing to be squashed.

Purdy Pavlova

The Pavlova, national dessert of Australia and New Zealand, is a meringue-based cake with a light, crisp crust and a soft, spongy inside. Pavlovas are often filled with whipped cream and topped with fruit or other sweet offerings.

TURDY PAVLOVA

FAIL

This cake's creator, Vondage, decided to pipe some leftover toffee onto her cake. The toffee was so difficult to control she gave up on perfection and just went for her name and a couple of sausage shapes.

Looks like turds. Tastes like toffee.

Milano Sheep Cookies

Last Easter, Kristen's father-in-law came across a project in a magazine and said to his wife, "What a fabulous thing for you to do with our granddaughter!" (Note: He did not volunteer himself for this effort.) The idea was simple: Make sheep from Milano cookies, melted almond bark, mini marshmallows, and mini chocolate chips.

MUTANT MILANO SHEEP

FAIL

Forget a cute wooly flock, these were genetically modified sheep cookies. The heads wouldn't stay on straight, the chocolate chips were too large, the marshmallows fell off, and none of the sheep could stand properly.

Kristen's mother-in-law kindly preserved a specimen in Tupperware. Score one point for science.

Darlene
It is now almost 5:00 a.m., and I am up reading this because I needed a laugh. I am sure the next time I am counting sheep, your mutant cookies will be there, probably eating the normal sheep.

Rainbow Gelatin Cake

Sarah was so impressed when she saw a layered rainbow gelatin that she knew she had to re-create it. After labor-intensive layering and chilling, hours of Sarah's day had disappeared to her task. She flipped the Bundt pan onto an antique cake plate. . . .

RAINBOW OF TERROR

The pot of gold at the end of this rainbow is that she is now exempt from bringing dishes to the church potluck.

Blockbuster Cupcakes

These beauties came from a cookbook, which means they were scientifically tested! But when a bit of radioactive flour fell into a batch of ready-made cake mix, the batter took on a life of its own. At first, everything looked fine and the cakes started to rise nicely, but then all of a sudden . . .

B-MOVIE HORROR CUPCAKES

. . . bubbling goo oozed everywhere, and these innocent chocolate cupcakes mutated into a horror from a 1950s creature feature.

Train Cake

Michelle and Sam's friend had always wanted a train cake for her birthday.

THE LITTLE CAKE THAT COULDN'T

FAIL

She said "train cake," not "train wreck."

Pretzel Bites

Julia wanted to make pretzel bites for an after-school snack.

FAIL

She ended up with little lady bits.

Halle
My mom actually did this; it worked. You probably just got careless. I should post a pic of hers.

Taste the Rainbow Cakes

From our CraftFail inbox, we've learned that nothing is more tempting to a crafter than a rainbow-colored dessert.

EPIC FAIL

THE INSOMNIA-INDUCED RAINBOW FAIL

PASTEL RAINBOW LAYER CAKE FAIL

Christina swears she followed each step correctly.

Karla's 18-year-old daughter bakes when she can't sleep. . . . Maybe sleep is the missing ingredient here.

UNICORN PARTY FOUL

OMBRE RAINBOW CAKE FAIL

Layering the cakes INSIDE the pan doesn't solve any problems. . . . It just looks like a unicorn puked up a rainbow.

Liz learned that using only one box of cake mix instead of two results in a Hobbit hole—shaped cake. (It's my eleventy-first birthday, and I want an ombre cake!)

FREEZING RAINBOW

Off to an excellent start, Desiree's cake layers turned out beautifully.

But they started to crack after assembly, so she placed the cake in the freezer in hopes of reinforcing the shifting layers. When she opened the door again . . . stone cold failure.

Birthday Cake

Brianne's friend, a first-time baker, set out to make her a birthday cake.

FAIL

She couldn't present the cake without an apology.

Cat Cakes

Marlene threw a birthday party for her cat one year and attempted some feline-inspired cake recipes she found in a magazine.

IT'S THE ICING ON THE CAT. . .

There's a reason why most people don't celebrate the birthdays of their cats.

Strawberry Cake Crush

Courtney saw this beautiful fresh strawberry cake and couldn't resist making one of her very own. She committed to following all the directions (even though she usually strayed), but sadly found out that the cake just wasn't that into her.

STRAWBERRY BREAK-UP CAKE

FAIL

The cake's middle had sunk in and the from-scratch frosting had the consistency of melted ice cream.

Then she cut into the cake to discover that, despite the red food coloring she added, the inside had faded to a gross marbled color. Don't worry, Courtney. There are plenty more fish in the sea.

Angry Bird Pizza

Michelle wanted to surprise her Angry Bird–fanatic husband after work with a fun pizza. Her Red Bird pepperoni pizza looked pretty darn good when she put it in to bake, so she confidently directed her husband to get his surprise out of the oven when he got home.

SAD BIRD PIZZA

FAIL

Surprise! It's a sad, cross-eyed, beakless mess.

Mini Caramel Apple Checklist

Use a melon baller to
cut rounds of apples.
Check.
Dry off the resulting apple
balls and dip them in caramel.
Check.
Roll the caramel apple
balls in sprinkles.
Check.
Watch all your efforts
slide off the apple balls?

MINI CARAMEL APPLE BLACKLIST

FAIL

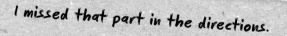

I missed that part in the directions.

14-Layer Crepe Cake

Erin stumbled upon a gorgeous photo of a 14-layer cake, and like any good Pinterest addict, she got the Pinterest rush, a condition in which an Internet enthusiast feels suddenly as if she could do anything she puts her mind to. She baked the cakes, layer after layer, in individual foil pans, for her father's birthday.

14 LAYERS OF FAIL

And they looked like pancakes. Pancakes covered in chocolate goo. (She nonetheless stuck a candle in it, sang "Happy Birthday," and then served it, layer by layer, flapjack-style.)

Rainbow Pinwheel Cookies

EPIC FAIL

Turning sugar cookies into beautiful rainbow swirls shouldn't be that hard, should it? They look so *playful,* like a kid could do it.

I WOULD NOT EAT THEM HERE OR THERE

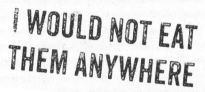

I WOULD NOT EAT THEM ANYWHERE

Oh! The places you'll fail!

Jen and Bethany: "It's harder than it looks."

Wendy: "Not quite the unicorn poop I was hoping for."

Flattened Chicken Breast:

Kim, OneClassyMotha.com

While working on a cooking "Tip for Tuesday" for my blog that didn't go quite as planned, I inadvertently developed a "Don't Try This at Home" Tip for Tuesday. I was preparing a delicious chicken dish (that I have made before) that calls for pounding the chicken breast to ⅛ inch thick. If you've ever done this, you know how hard it can be. Ten minutes and one numb hand later, I managed to get one breast flattened. I still had six to go. I thought, *Surely there must be an easier way.* Then, as a DIY, think-outside-the-box kinda girl, I had the most brilliant idea ever!

How Not to Pound Chicken:

1. Place chicken breasts between two large pieces of wax paper.

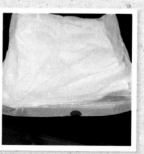

2. Carefully slide the breasts into a garbage bag, then double bag with another garbage bag.

Don't Try This Tip for Tuesday

3. Keeping the trash bag o' chicken horizontal, slide it onto a cookie sheet and transport it outside.

4. Place the garbage bag on the ground in front of your car wheel.

FAIL

6. Here's where the story shifts into—ahem—high gear. Hear the bag pop and watch chicken breasts fly onto the driveway (and into the garbage).

7. Order pizza.

5. Gently roll over the bag with your car while asking your kids if you're "on it yet." Forward, reverse, forward, reverse, and so forth.

8. Find your husband laughing at the YouTube video of you "cooking dinner."

9. Thank your son for mercilessly capturing the entire fiasco on his iPod and sending it to Tosh.O.

Cinnamon Pull-Apart Bread

Fatimah couldn't wait to make this cinnamon pull-apart bread for a new and interesting take on traditional cinnamon rolls. Putting it together was surprisingly easy. Or so she thought, until it came out of the oven . . .

CINNAMON FALL-APART BREAD

FAIL

. . . looking like a science experiment gone wrong.

Spaghetti-Stuffed Garlic Bread

Summer wanted to make the spaghetti baked in garlic bread recipe she found on Pinterest. She assembled it, then wrestled the unwieldy, slippery, stretchy wet mess from the counter onto a baking sheet, slid it into the oven, and hoped for the best.

ALIEN-AUTOPSY GARLIC BREAD

FAIL

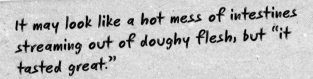

It may look like a hot mess of intestines streaming out of doughy flesh, but "it tasted great."

Erin H.
OMG I cannot stop laughing out loud. My dogs are barking at me and my husband just told me to stop because I am scaring the kids!

Peppermint Divinity

When Heather saw a microwave recipe for Peppermint Divinity, she was inspired (who wouldn't be?) and thought confidently, *I can handle this.* Cue the harps and angel choir.

PEPPERMINT PROFANITY

But when she opened the infernal regions of her microwave, what, pray tell, emerged from its hell-mouth?

Kate
I think they resemble speech bubbles. You could place them near gingerbread men with phrases like "Nailed it!" spelled out in Alpha-Bits cereal. Another craft project!

Melted Snowman Cookies

During a particularly obsessive search for cute food on Pinterest, Rylee found a few pictures of very adorable "melted snowmen" cookies. She was hot to try them.

SNOWMAN COOKIE MELTDOWN

FAIL

The scarves and arms became one, the faces melted into terrifying leers like the baddies' faces at the end of Raiders of the Lost Ark. And one of them was wearing a red bikini?

Emily
Uh-oh . . . I was planning on trying these this weekend for a bake sale on Monday.

Carrie
I love how the one in the bikini looks like her makeup is running.

Cupcakes Are Easy

EPIC FAIL

What's trendy, shareable, and looks easier than baking a whole cake? Cupcakes! Well, the key word here is *looks*. Cupcakes may be delicious and adorable, but they're just darn hard to bake! Too bad that the trend is never going away. . .

CAKE A MESS

Do they make Spanx for cupcake pans?

GO AHEAD, CUPCAKE MY DAY

I know what you're thinking, punk. You're thinking: "Is that actual cupcake batter, or is it something much nastier?" So you've gotta ask yourself a question: Do you feel lucky? Well, do ya, punk?

FAKE IT 'TIL YOU CUPCAKE IT

Even if you look like a misshapen glop of lumpy batter, call yourself a cupcake anyway.

Eggs in a Heart-Shaped Basket

One morning Carey decided to make some lovely Eggs in a Basket: Cut a hole, pour in the egg, cook, enjoy! Right?

ANATOMICAL HEART ON TOAST

FAIL

I don't think that's the heart shape Carey was going for.

Macarons

Oh, that darling pastel-colored French cookie with the name that doesn't look quite right (plus there's no coconut in them, which is really confusing for Americans). They're *très* difficult to make, but when Becky first saw macarons make an appearance on *MasterChef,* she knew she had to give the recipe a try.

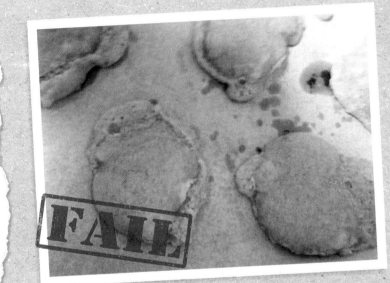

It's pronounced "Craparoons."

Callum Hann's kitchen:
I found this funny blog where someone made my macarons from #masterchefau.

Cake Pops

EPIC FAIL

I'm a big fan of Bakerella: She basically invented the cake pop and has managed to turn a single culinary item into an empire, with merchandise (cake pop kits, anyone?) and a regular gig in the Starbucks pastry case. (Does she get 7 cents for every cake pop sold?)

She also makes it look so darn easy to plop balls of cake mixed with frosting onto a stick, and then decorate them to look like photo-realistic Muppets or U.S. presidents—appropriate for any occasion!

A DELIGHTFUL MOTHER'S DAY TREAT

FOR INDEPENDENCE DAY

Happy Mother's Day, Mom! I made you something!

Three cheers for the pink, brown, and blue.

FOR YOUR DOG'S BIRTHDAY

Toi: "Overfill your cake pop pan and they're guaranteed to come out looking like crap."

IT'S BEGINNING TO LOOK A LOT LIKE CHRISTMAS CAKE POPS

LIKE A CAKE POP VIRGIN

Looks like someone's on the naughty list.

Megan: "Don't ever have a first time making cake pops. Because it never ends well."

Shark Week Cupcakes

Although she created three picture-perfect shark cakes, LeAna admitted that they were the hardest cupcakes she'd ever made and could go no further.

SHARK WEAK CUPCAKES

FAIL

Vicki attempted the challenging cupcakes anyway, after her 6-year-old begged for them.

You're gonna need a bigger trash can.

Chapter 5

MARTHA MADE IT

Martha Stewart, today's undisputed reigning queen of the domestic, is the empress of the four pillars of the creative home: cooking, crafting, gardening, and decorating. Every month in her magazine, Martha personally demonstrates how she celebrates holidays, makes gorgeous flower arrangements, crafts up quick and easy "good things," and cooks delicious food.

Everything about Martha's World is aspirational, which means it is designed to make readers want to be like her. Sure, an average crafter can aspire to fold an exquisite 1,000-point origami star just like Martha's, but the results can be disappointing on the first try. Or the ninth.

For anyone who has ever tried a Martha craft and craftfailed, this chapter is for you.

With a Name Like "Scherenschnitte," It's Gotta Be Easy

Heather's imagination was captured when she saw the cover of *Martha Stewart Living* featuring German folk art-style paper cutout Easter eggs. *I WILL make those eggs,* she thought.

MARTHA'S SCHADENFREUDE

This craft had the trifecta: tricky-to-cut paper patterns, impossible-to-mix robin's egg blue dye, tedious-to-make blown eggs.

Simple, not so much.

T-Shirt Necklace

Megan was searching for fun crafts to do with her nieces, when she came across the "T-Shirt Necklace" on the almighty MarthaStewart.com. It looked easy enough. Heck, it looked like something she could crank out during a commercial break of *Touched By An Angel*!

T-SHIRT NECKLACE TRANSGRESSION

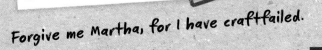

Forgive me Martha, for I have craftfailed.

Tissue Pom-Poms

A perfect puff of pom-pom. They look so simple. And yet . . . Aunt Peaches, craft blogger, confesses: "I cannot make Martha's famous tissue poms. Probably the easiest, most popular, and most readily available craft idea on the Internet, tissue poms involve nothing more than tissue paper and a simple accordion fold. And yet, I cannot make them. At least, I cannot make them look nice."

FLATTENED FLOWER

MANGLED MOTH

They come out squashed and torn and look like something one might use to scrub feet.

Aunt Peaches
Sad face.

WINDBLOWN WAD

It's a tissue paper butterfly—yeah, that's the ticket.

kelly: "Less than thrilled with my fistful of tissue"

SO EASY A KID CAN DO IT

me

I got a pre-made Martha Stewart tissue pom-pom pumpkin kit, and even this kit, wherein almost EVERYTHING was already made, resulted in a rumpled tissue-paper mess. I failed, but my seven-year-old son managed to make them look good.

Vallen Q.
You're just making the folds too big is all. Fold six sheets in 1-inch pleats. Secure the middle with a twisty tie, round off the ends with scissors (or points at the ends are cute, too), then slowly, gently, and with small ladylike movements, peel each sheet toward the middle. Fouf. The fouffing part is kind of important. You will be an expert at this in no time and be making the best tissue pom-poms in the world. Remember: fouf.

Martha's Translucent Pumpkin Carving

Jessica was inspired by Martha Stewart's translucent pumpkin tutorial, in which you carve away the opaque skin of the pumpkin to reveal an elegant design.

SEEING THROUGH MARTHA'S TRANSLUCENT PUMPKIN CARVING

Jessica attempted the craft with a faux pumpkin. Newsflash: Faux pumpkins are made of opaque foam.

Eggshell Votives

Carissa just *knew* that her spent egg shells had useful craft potential, so she was thrilled when she found Martha's idea to make votive candles out of real eggshells. Keeping with the re-use theme, Carissa even melted down some leftover candle wax.

ROTTEN EGG VOTIVES

FAIL

Recycled eggshells + recycled wax = straight into the trash.

Martha's Ombre Candles

Heidi found Martha's ombre dipped candle idea on Pinterest—just melt down some crayons for a pretty, understated effect.

DEXTER BLOOD SPATTERED CANDLES

The project was much more violent than she expected: No matter how small she chopped the pieces of crayons, they never completely melted, even after a full hour in a double boiler. The final insult: a stinky mess of globby wax that stained her hands red when she tried to clean it up.

Martha's Waxed Hearts

EPIC FAIL

I remember when these wax paper hearts were published in *Martha Stewart Living* circa 1999. I immediately made them and stuck them up in my window. You know, suncatchers made out of wax paper and crayons. Because *everyone* wants flimsy, waxy hearts that look like melted Rorschach tests hanging in their windows.

MARTHA'S WAXED HEARTBREAKERS

Laura: "Tried to save my wax hearts fail. Ended up with heart-shaped poop."

HOW RORSCHACH-ING!

Amy: "I see a murderous seahorse."

WAX ON . . . WAX <u>SO</u> OFF.

Sam: "Iron ruined. Send reinforcements."

Martha's Bath Bombs

Mary was inspired to make some effervescent bath bombs that she found on MarthaStewart.com.

FAIL

When they didn't come out as well as she expected, Mary put the failed balls in a vase, then didn't think about them for two weeks. By the time she remembered her failure, the balls were cemented into the vase.

Chapter 6

KIDS. CRAFTS. FAILS.

Kids are the inspiration for a lot of crafting that goes on in the world. Many of the most ridiculous and pointless crafts were created as a way to keep our holy terrors busy for just a few minutes. Under the influence of online inspiration boards, many moms feel guilty if they don't regularly do cutesy crafts with their spawn. And despite our best intentions, those kids' crafts often don't turn out as cute as they should. Join us as we preserve our babies' piggies in sludgy playdough, accidentally feed our sons and daughters soapy water, and fail to tame the mythical rubber band loom monster.

Microwave Soap Fluff

Did you know if you microwave a bar of soap, it explodes into soap fluff? The photo of a boy playing with soap fluff has become iconic on Pinterest. People see it, see the tagline "microwave soap fluff" and figure they have all the info they need (action, object, result!). However, you do actually need to know *one tiny* detail.*

MICROWAVE SOAP SLUDGE

FAIL

How did the cat manage to vomit in the microwave?

*Only one kind of soap bar will work: Ivory.

Baby Foot Memory Print

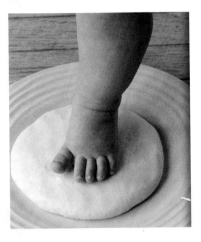

When Emily saw the simple salt-dough baby footprint keepsake online, she *knew* she had to immortalize her baby's tootsies in salt-dough, too.

BABY FOOT FORGET IT PRINT

FAIL

This is the true record of how a baby foot behaves when exposed to sticky dough.

What Does the Fox Say?

Katie loves foxes so, naturally, she wanted to create her own stuffed felt animal.

HOW DOES THE FOX FAIL?

FAIL

when you meet a friendly fail, will you tell it to go to hay-hay-hay-hay-hell?

Bubble Snakes

Stephanie found this activity on Pinterest: Bubble Snakes. Wrap a sock around the cut end of a plastic water bottle, and secure it with a rubber band. Dip the sock into a soap solution and blow into the mouth of the bottle, creating a long "snake" of bubbles. Once she assembled it, Stephanie handed the contraption to her 6-year-old son. He put it to his lips. And breathed in.

BURP BUBBLES

A moment later, he was foaming at the mouth. Bubbles actually floated out of his mouth like you see in cartoons.

Jellyfish in a Bottle

Linda loves making cute crafts for her toddler to play with, and was inspired by a clever jellyfish-in-a-bottle craft, in which a plastic bag is turned into a jellyfish that floats effortlessly in an upcycled drink bottle.

JIMMY HAT IN A BOTTLE

FAIL

Linda's version turned out to be rated M for Mature.

May the Craft Be with You

Lynda wanted to dress her baby up as a certain popular Jedi Master for Halloween. She picked the green-eared hat up at the costume shop, but she decided to knit up some quick three-toed socks to really get the look right.

FAIL OR FAIL NOT, THERE IS NO TRY

This little Yoda can only count to five.

FAIL

Once Lynda headed down the path of the craftfail dark side, forever did it dominate her sock-knitting destiny.

Yoda
Starting too late the night before leads to anger; using too little yarn leads to frustration; knitting only two toes on one foot leads to one big #CraftFail.

DAD'S DAY DECORATION DISASTER

For Father's Day, Tracy and her two preschool sons created a memory plaque to give to the man of the house.

How do you spell "FAIL" backward?

Perler Bead Magic

Perler Beads are small plastic beads that can be arranged on a pegboard and then fused together using a protective wax paper layer and an iron. Favored by geek crafters because of their resemblance to pixel art, Perler Beads are a versatile craft supply enjoyed by kids of all ages.

PERLER BEAD MELTDOWN

FAIL

This is what happens when a Perler shape gets stuck to your iron and you don't notice for a while.

Bathtub Crayon Soap

While developing a recipe for bathtub puffy paint, Regina dried the soap paint in a mold, in the hopes that it would harden into a bathtub crayon. Thinking heat might speed up the drying process, Regina put them in the oven for a few minutes. Huge mistake.

CUPID'S ANATOMY SOAP

Did we say huge mistake? More like teeny, tiny mistake.

Rachelle D.
You know there's someone out there trying to figure out how to make phallic bathtub crayons, and you've just saved them a bunch of time!

Jo
Those crayons are hawt!!!

Rubber Band Loom Octopus

Rubber band looms took the tween crafting world by storm in 2013, and soon kids across the world were weaving more than just rubber band bracelets. This amazing rubber band octopus creation captured Claire's imagination.

RUBBER BAND LOOM CHTHULU

FAIL

Here's Claire's version. She calls it "Rubber Band Loom Flying Spaghetti Monster."

International Hula Hoop Weaving

EPIC FAIL

According to *Family Fun* magazine, you can use a hula hoop as a large circular frame for a round weaving project. A woven rug made on a hula hoop? Sign me up!

Our international network of crafty field agents reports that the weaving project isn't as simple as it appears. Many crafty agents botched weaving projects to get us this information.

HULA HOOP WEAVING—
IT'S A TRAP!

HULA HOOP WEAVING—
ES UN SOMBRERO!

Aimee's rug looked great as she was weaving it, but she said, "I could see the trouble as I started to clip the edges."

¡Ai-yi-yi! SoShawna's rug turned into a sombrero. Or a serving bowl for chips and salsa.

Aimee
My rag rug is now a rag bowl.

HULA HOOP WEAVING— IT'S A TAM!

CROUCHING WEAVING, HIDDEN HULA HOOP HAT

yes mon, Summer made the rug too, irie.

Casey's fail took on an Asian flavor.

Summer
My daughter promptly used it as a RastaCap.

Casey
It's a rice paddy hat made out of woven T-shirts!

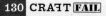

Little Cutie Sensory Bottle

Alyssa, in pursuit of creative mom points, saw these sensory jars online and thought, *Fill water bottles with stuff and water? I can do this! My kid will be mesmerized for hours!* In a clever streak all her own, she hot-glued the top on after tightening it. Mistake.

FAIL

Inadvertent lint remover!

It leaked. The sticky label adhesive made the bottle a trap for loose hair. Great for preschoolers!

> **Heather**
> *Sticky* is part of sensory play, right?

The Caped Crusader

Gotham's craft halls are crying out for a crusader. A craft crusader who is capable of creating a halfway decent-looking Batman mask for a kid's Halloween costume.

THE CRAPPED CRUSADER

FAIL

A couple of uneven bat ears and a non-eye-reaching mask with misshapen holes should do the trick.

Commissioner Gordon
This is the hat Batman deserves, but not the one he needs right now.

Excellent Way to Recycle Easter Eggs

Make a fun toy out of Easter Egg halves—all you need is some glue and a couple of googly eyes.

X-RATED WAY TO RECYCLE EASTER EGGS

Different kind of snake . . .

Looks like somebody raided the Easter Bunny's nightstand.

Friendship Bracelet

Many teens go through a friendship bracelet-making phase—they spend hours with embroidery floss macrame projects clipped to their jeans.

FAILSHIP BRACELET

FAIL

Some friendships just aren't meant to be.

Allison
KIT. JK. Don't.

Chapter 7

A FOR EFFORT.

Sometimes you do everything right. Except that one thing. Whether it's using fabric you have on hand instead of what is recommended, making do with the wrong tool, or forgetting to read *just one* word in the instructions, sometimes, despite your best intentions, it just ends up wrong. Some prefer to skim the directions, others view crafting rules as more of what you'd call "guidelines," or are paralyzed with performance anxiety—it's not always the craft's fault. We hope you'll find some kindred craftfailers among our collection of right crafts gone wrong.

WHAT A STRONG SEWING MACHINE YOU HAVE THERE

"I thought I felt a little extra something while I was sewing."

Cut Bottle Hack

A throwback to the crafty heyday of the 1970s, cut glass bottles are called an "easy and addictive" craft by Pinterest fanatics. The hack? Soak yarn in acetone, tie it around a glass bottle where you want to break it, light the yarn on fire, wait till it burns out, and dunk the bottle in cold water.

BOTTLES THAT WILL CUT YOU

Jennifer attacked a bottle of Two Buck Chuck. She found the yarn and acetone process addictive, but after five tries, there was no apparent effect on the wine bottle. Easy? Not so much.

On the sixth try, she finally got the wine bottle to crack—into a jagged, unusable mess.

Sweet Crocheted Mouse

Laura was excited to try out a cute beginner amigurumi crocheted mouse pattern.

BITTER CROCHETED MOUSE

FAIL

Laura called her version of the toy "a psychedelic shrew."

THERE'S NO SPELLCHECK IN CROSS-STITCH

How many hours did Diana spend on her misspelled cross-stitch before she noticed her error?

Homemade Glitter: Taking an Idea from Concept to Fail

Steve Hoefer, grathio.com

One day, I was minding my own business when lightning struck. Glitter lightning. *Wouldn't it be great if you could get fresh-made glitter, on demand?* I imagined a glitter pepper mill. I'd be able to adjust the color, style, and coarseness on the fly. I imagined a world where perfect glitter was a right, not a privilege.

Nevermind that. I haven't worked with glitter since I was ten. And, frankly, I'm not particularly fond of it. That's why I needed Pat, my sister. "Let's give it a try!" was her response when I tried to enlist her help. She's almost as crazy as I am and has an affinity for the sparkly stuff. With the team assembled, the project was on.

We knew that most commercial glitter is made of chopped up sheets of metalized plastic and some of the higher end stuff is actually glass. What more do you need to know? So we headed out to the thrift store to pick up a couple pepper grinders and some grindable raw materials. We ended up with poker chips, glass and plastic Christmas ornaments, some children's jewelry, mosaic glass, and various other brightly colored plastic things. Sounds promising, right?

Preparation:

It took us one short afternoon to completely obliterate both grinders, so the dream of pulling your faithful old glitter mill out of your toolbox any time you need custom glitter was shot. It's more of a one-time-use option.

Analysis:

Plastic Christmas Ornaments

I had high hopes for these because they're made of metalized plastic, which (I thought) should produce results similar to standard glitter. Turns out once the metalized surface comes off, you have a lot of white plastic underneath. Not exactly what we were hoping for.

Result: faux dandruff

Plastic Poker Chips

The hard plastic was much better for grinding and the texture ended up being good, but there's nothing particularly sparkly in a poker chip. Hmm, should've thought of that.

Result: pile of dirt

Continued →

Plastic Pencil Sharpener

We thought for sure this brightly colored monstrosity would produce some passable glitter. We were wrong.

Result: lime pop rocks

Plastic Miniature Hair Clips

This is where we started cheating. These beautiful, delicate butterflies had glitter already embedded in them. But the rough edges produced by the grinder removed even the shine they started with.

Result: butterfly massacre

Glass Christmas Ornaments

These were dangerous but the easiest to grind. Only a small amount of blood was spilled, but we did produce a frightening pile of powdered glass. We also came the closest to achieving our dream scenario: We could mix colors and the result was sparkly (but sharp).

Result: lethal glitter

Mosaic Glass

This stuff is essentially floor sweepings from a stained-glass factory. None of it is particularly sparkly, but it was still more interesting than any of the plastic options. Still, not exactly *glitter.* And it completely destroyed both pepper mills.

Result: jagged little jewels

FAIL

Glass glitter on a baby shoe, what could possibly go wrong?

Conclusion:

Technically, we succeeded in making a glitterlike product using pepper mills and inexpensive household items, but all of the acceptably sparkly results were made from crushed glass. Which is kind of horribly dangerous. Which is apparently why we decided to decorate a pair of baby shoes with it.

This project had all the makings of an ideal craft experiment: frustration, danger, disappointment, and some final products that require an OSHA team to dispose of safely. We haven't given up on the dream of one day creating custom glitter on demand, but we do have a new appreciation for the premade stuff.

Maybe if I used a coffee grinder. . . .

CALL IN THE BATH BOMB SQUAD

When she formed them and placed them into a cupcake tin, Jennifer's bath balls started to rise and spread out. In an attempt to defuse the situation, she placed the fizzing bombs in cupcake liners and then put them in the oven on the lowest temperature, hoping to draw out some moisture.

Twenty minutes went by, and then: BOOM.

WARNING:
MAY CONTAIN
EXPLOSIVES!

Heather
Whose idea was it to bake a bomb, anyway?

DIY Screenprinting

Samantha read on the Internet that you can screenprint using tights and an embroidery hoop, and because she owns lots of tights and lots of embroidery hoops, she decided to try it.

SCREENPRINTING SPLODGE

FAIL

The result: total craft choke. No design (unless you count inkblots as a design), and for the final insult, the fabric paint went right through to the dining room table underneath!

Pinterest-Inspired Scarf Organizer

All you need to make a dandy scarf organizer is a hanger and some dollar-store shower curtain rings.

FAIL

LEAN TO THE LEFT,

LEAN TO THE RIGHT....

what, you wanted it to stay balanced, too?

Star-Crossed Ceramic Story

MO'SAIC MO'PROBLEMS

so meta...

Ana was at the local thrift store when she spotted a cute little ceramic tile with a folk art bird design on it and fell in love with it—the style, the colors—instantly. Some love stories are doomed from the start, however: On her way home from the thrift store, the tile broke into many itty bitty pieces. Saddened, but willing to pick up the pieces (literally), she decided to salvage the situation and make a mosaic.

After the mosaic was complete, disaster struck (AGAIN). Burning question: Does anyone know how to make a mosaic out of a broken mosaic?

Molded Marigolds

In an attempt to make some flower pins inspired by some in the Anthropologie catalog, Johnnie placed a candy mold in the oven.

FAIL

Ten minutes and one very funny smell later, she learned that candy molds aren't heat resistant.

Soft Yarn Trick

Allyson saw a pin on Pinterest enticing her to "make your scratchy acrylic yarn soft!" She got several skeins of acrylic yarn and followed the extensive directions to loosen the yarn: Put it in a pillow case and tie it up, wash it in cold water with lots of fabric softener, and finally put it in the dryer on the fluff cycle.

SOFT YARN, TANGLED

The pin didn't come with instructions for detangling six skeins of hopelessly entwined yarn.

STEP AWAY FROM THE SEWING MACHINE

Sometimes you just gotta know when to take a break from quilting.

THE DOG ATE MY CRAFTFAIL

FAIL

"Oh, ur home. wuz jus doin' some krafz."

PUTTING THE IRON IN IRON-ON TRANSFER

Jen tried to apply one-step heat transfer vinyl to a bag that she bought from the dollar store.

CAT IN THE FELTED HAT

After two successful felted hat projects, Amy got brave and, instead of felting by hand, decided to felt in the washing machine.

The result was a hat that no human could wear.

DESPERATE MEASURES

Um... That's not a pizza cutter...

When Lindsay's husband couldn't find the pizza cutter, he raided her craft supply stash and found her rotary cutter. Her next sewing project is going to smell *really* nice.

Nice Felted Scarf

Jenn took a freeform crochet class and was so inspired by the teacher's gorgeous wool scarf creations that were knitted and then felted in the washer.

NOOSE FELTED SCARF

FAIL

When Jenn removed her attempt from the washer, she found that it had fused together. To salvage her creation, Jenn tried to cut it apart, but her snipping resulted in a nooselike loop in the top of the scarf.

Now that's a scarf no one wants to wear.

Sharpie Mug

EPIC FAIL

The Sharpie Mug first came on the scene in a big way through the popular lifestyle blog *A Beautiful Mess*. The project, published in June 2012 as "His and Hers Sharpie Mugs," became a viral hit on Pinterest, and many crafters attempted to replicate the project the world over.

Although Elsie and Emma can do no wrong, their followers, it appears, *can*—and how!

SPOILER ALERT: Don't put your Sharpie Mug anywhere near a dishwasher.

I'M SORRY, I MUSTACHE YOU TO TRY AGAIN

DON'T BOTHER READING DIRECTIONS, IT'S OBVIOUS WHAT TO DO

Philip tried to use the Sharpie Mug technique to make a birthday present for his friend who has a mustache and soul patch.

It's a common trait of craftfailers: doing a project without reading the actual instructions.

MY LOVE FOR YOU IS FADING

Randi initially had good luck with her Sharpie mug, making sure to only hand-wash. For months she deemed it a success—until some disgraceful person put it in the dishwasher.

The Immortal Sharpie Mug

Tips, in case you DO decide to make a Sharpie Mug:

- Cheap mugs fare better because of their inferior glaze (all the better to stain you with, my dear). Check the dollar store or other discount stores.

- Before applying your Sharpie design, clean the mug with rubbing alcohol and allow to dry. This will clean any residue off the mug that could interfere with the design.

- To set the ink onto the mug, cure the mug. Set it in a cold oven, and heat the oven to 450°F, then let it bake for 30 minutes. Turn the oven off and leave the mug in there until the oven cools completely.

- Hand-wash only, with no abrasives. These mugs are *not* dishwasher safe.

- If all this mug mollycoddling sounds like too much work, use a pen that was designed to work on ceramic in the first place, such as a Pebeo Porcelaine marker, or apply a design with glass paints (such as Martha Stewart Glass Paints), and make sure to follow the package directions.

Simply Stenciled Pillow

Carissa read a blog post that recommended using stencils to breathe new life into an old throw pillow. Following conventional wisdom, she put a bird on it.

PUT A BLOB ON IT

Quoth the pillow "Nevermore."

FAIL

Contributors and Credits

Thanks to our failers, who documented and submitted their spectacular craftfails and made this book possible. And thanks to the people whose inspirational projects were featured in this book.

CRAFT INSPIRATION PHOTOS:

Home Decor Fails

Page 9: Papier Mâché Animal Bust, WhiteFauxTaxidermy.com

Page 10: Insanely Easy No-Sew Pillow Cover, Leanne Jacobs, organizeyourstuffnow.com

Page 12: The Beautiful Button Bowl, Kristen Tool

Page 14: Darling 3-Dimensional Wall Art, Virginia Saint, virginiaandcharlie.blogspot.com

Page 15: Melted Crayon Canvas Rainbow, Stephanie Nuccitelli, 52kitchenadventures.com

Page 16: Paint Chip Collage, Crystal Owens

Fashion Fails

Page 24: The 20-Minute T-Shirt Dress, Meg Churray, tripoverjoy.com

Page 25: Fashion with Scissors, Model: Shannon Oberg

Page 27: Woven Scarf Wars, Catie Morgan, Sassafras Fiber Arts, sassafrassfiberarts.etsy.com

Page 29: Union Jack Knit Cap, Melissa Lucier/ Workman Publishing (photo). Model: Ariana Abud

Page 34: Ink Stain Shirt, Model: Annie Bailey

Page 35: Glinda's Glitter Shoes, ©iStock.com/jurden

Page 36: Marbled Nail Art, Jodi Davis, captivatingclaws.blogspot.com

Page 40: The Magic Marble Manicure, Jodi Davis, captivatingclaws.blogspot.com

Holiday Fails

Page 43: Toilet Paper Tube Wreath, Trish Flake and Bonnie Mauney, uncommondesignsonline.com

Page 47: Stained-Glass-Window Cookies, Noema Pérez, interculturayocinaenglish.blogspot.de

Page 49: Betty's Bunny Cake, Holly Malkin

Page 50: Oreo Reindeer Pops, Jamie Harrison, mommasfabulousplayground.blogspot.com

Page 53: Intricate Easter Eggs, ©iStock.com/ step2626

Page 54: Pumpkin Glitter Greatness, Anna Sandler, randomhandprints.com

Page 57: Día de los Muertos Sugar Skull, Alex Barth, flickr.com/photos/a-barth

Page 58: Turkey Cookie, Elizabeth Boncich, lizybbakes.blogspot.com

Page 60: The Rickrack Flag Shirt, Aurelia Good, ourgoodfamily.org

Page 61: Witch Finger Cookies, ©iStock.com/ kongxinzhu

Food Fails

Page 68: Rainbow Cake in a Jar, Brooke McLay, cheekykitchen.com

Page 70: Melted Marshmallow Frosting, Crystal Owens

Page 72: Purdy Pavlova, ©iStock.com/ola_p

Page 73: Milano Sheep Cookies, Carolyn Garris

Page 74: Rainbow Gelatin Cake, ©iStock.com/ Andrea Skjold

Page 75: Blockbuster Cupcakes, ©iStock.com/ Chris_Elwell

Page 76: Train Cake, Holly Malkin

Page 77: Pretzel Bites, ©iStock.com/magnez2

Page 78: Taste the Rainbow Cakes, ©iStock.com/ Siraphol

Page 83: Cat Cakes, Holly Malkin

Page 84: Strawberry Cake Crush, ©iStock.com/ Elenathewise

Page 85: Angry Bird Pizza, Carolyn Garris

Page 86: Mini Caramel Apple Checklist, Jared Mann

Page 87: 14-Layer Crepe Cake, Holly Malkin

Page 88: Rainbow Pinwheel Cookies, Holly Malkin

Page 92: Cinnamon Pull-Apart Bread, Melissa Mondragon

Page 93: Spaghetti-Stuffed Garlic Bread, Melissa Mondragon

Page 95: Melted Snowman Cookies, Megan Dulgarian, somewhatsimple.com

Page 96: Cupcakes Are Easy, ©iStock.com/ melissasanger

Page 98: Eggs in a Heart-Shaped Basket, Carey Nershi, reclaimingprovincial.com

Page 99: Macarons, ©iStock.com/RuthBlack

Page 100: Cake Pops, ©iStock.com/RuthBlack

Page 104: Shark Week Cupcakes, LeAna K., asmallsnippet.com

Martha Made It

Page 106: With a Name Like "Scherenschnitte," It's Gotta Be Easy, Jill Fritz, createcraftlove.com

Page 107: T-Shirt Necklace, Model: Shannon Oberg

Page 108: Tissue Pom-Poms, Stacy Molter, stacymolter.com

Page 114: Martha's Waxed Hearts, Carolyn Garris

Page 116: Martha's Bath Bombs, ©iStock.com/ HeikeRau

Kids. Crafts. Fails.

Page 118: Microwave Soap Fluff, Crystal Owens

Page 119: Baby Foot Memory Print, Charlie Ostrander, attemptingaloha.com

Page 122: Jellyfish in a Bottle, Jatuporn Tansirimas, bhoomplay.wordpress.com

Page 125: Perler Bead Magic, Julie K. Gray

Page 128: International Hula Hoop Weaving, Alexandra Grablewski, agrablewski.com

Page 131: Little Cutie Sensory Bottle, Carolyn Garris

Home Decor Fails

Page 8: Love Me or Wreath Me, Iuliana Blakely, hip2thrift.com

Page 9: Busted Papier Mâché Animal, Meg Padgett, revamphomegoods.com

Page 10: Insanity-Inspired Pillow Cover, Melissa Taylor and Leanne Jacobs, melissataylorphotography.com

Page 11: A Little Piece of Chevron, Michelle Beaton, Weekendcraft.com

Page 13: Popped a Button Bowl, Juliet Elizabeth; Blown Button Bowl, Madison Olp, planetmads.com; Penny Dreadful Fail, Christine L. Leahy, letsgetcrafty.org, womenstandup.net

Page 14: Oh, Deer, 3-Dimensional Art?, Emily H.

Page 15: Melted Crayon Canvas Inferno, Courtney McCaughley

Page 16: Paint Chip Fail-age, Alyssa Wine, myclevernest.com

Page 17: Paisley Poo-Brella, Michelle Lichter, MichLinLA.com

Page 19: Gravity Balls, Shannon Madigan, madiganmade.com; If These Balls Could Talk, Amy Anderson, modpodgerocksblog.com

Page 20: Botched Balloon Animal Balls, Carla Maggi; Great Balls of Failure, Amanda Hendrix, loveandrenovations.com

Page 21: Cry Me a Glitter, Lauren Lanker, thinkingcloset.com; No Rest for the Shriveled, Haley Morrison; Try, Try Again, Tracy Boogerd

Page 22: Plaster Mask Planter Mush, Jenn Alvin, illusionaire.com

Fashion Fails

Page 24: DIY Sister Wife T-Shirt Dress, Jenna, Ali, and Nikki, everythingiwantandnothingidont.blogspot.com

Page 25: Failing with Scissors, Tess Kuhn

Page 26: These Are Spray-Painted Shoes on Crack, Jessica Underwood, adayinthelifeofonegirl.blogspot.com

Page 27: Amish-Dala's Headscarf Strikes Back, Korinne Zimmerman, Crafterella.com

Page 28: Downton Abbey Don't, Shannon Madigan

Page 29: Union Jack Cranium Cozy, Kelly Green and Sandra Signe Schmitke

Page 30: How Do You Spell Mommmy?, Brandy Yamamoto, maxandotis.com

Page 31: The Great Frankenstein Westwood Miscalculation, Carmen Bouchard-Salvan, Martial Salvan (photo), carmencitab.com

Page 32: Scarfing Some Bacon, Amanda, dailyamigurumi.blogspot.com

Page 33: Ginormous Shower Cap, Melissa Lucier/ Workman Publishing (photo). Model: Sarah Smith

Page 34: Pink Stain Shirt, Carla Moran, carladmoran.blogspot.com

Page 35: There's No Place Like Fail, Lindsey Harper

Page 37: Capture the Bag, Gina Xavier, on3d4y.blogspot.com

Page 38: Drip Tease, Sonja Foust, pintester.com; Nails from the Crypt, Stephanie Halligan, itfeelslikethefirsttime.com

Holiday Fails

Page 42: Polar Plunge, Lindsay Wolsey, allergictoparrots.blogspot.com

Page 43: Down the Toilet Paper Tube Wreath, Maddie Donily

Page 44: Freudian Carrot, Amanda Formaro, craftsbyamanda.com

Page 45: Possessed Peppermint Wreath, Brittany Bailey

Page 46: Christmas Tree Plaque Fail, Cathie Filian, handmadehappyhour.com

Page 47: Broken-Glass-Window Cookies, Tracy Meyer

Page 48: Peppermint Platter Puddle, Kristin Rushing

Page 49: Bad Bunny Cake, Shelly Howe

Page 50: Oreo Reindeer Plops, Carrie Norris

Page 51: Reindeer Marshmallow Duds, Iliana Castaneda

Page 52: Nuclear Chicken Meltdown, Jennifer Dyer

Page 53: Easter Egg Dropout, Madelyn Wischmeyer

Page 54: Pumpkin's Gotta Give, Anna Sandler, randomhandprints.com

Page 55: Gingerbread House of Horrors, Inspired by William and Demetra Brege

Page 56: Ant-y Easter Bouquet, Sarah Potts

Page 57: Día de los Fails, Dianna Busby

Page 58: Total Turkey, Alissa Julius

Page 59: Turkey Cookie Curlers, Jennifer Joseph

Page 60: The Rickrack Attack Shirt, Gina

Page 61: Smashed Witch Finger Cookies, Shoni Glanville

Page 62: The Red Reindeer Massacre, Kim from oneclassymotha.com

Page 63: Pumpkin Wicked This Way Comes, Alexa Westerfield Wolff, swelldesigner.com

Food Fails

Page 68: Napalm Cake in a Jar, Olivia Murphy

Page 69: Hole-Baked Bread, Erika Tindall

Page 71: The Melted Marshmallow Mutiny, Rachel Edwards

Page 72: Turdy Pavlova, Siobhan (Vondage)

Page 73: Mutant Milano Sheep, Kristen Tabor

Page 74: Rainbow of Terror, Sarah, Sarahbelle42.Etsy.com

Page 75: B-Movie Horror Cupcakes, Cassie Leedham

Page 76: The Little Cake That Couldn't, Michelle Bergeron and Sam Fleckenstein

Page 77: Pruh-Jay-Jays, Julia Terpstra, bles-id.blogspot.com

Page 79: The Insomnia-Induced Rainbow Fail,

Karla Traxel, workschoolkids.blogspot.com;
Pastel Layer Cake Fail, Cristina Leduc

Page 80: Unicorn Party Foul, Jessii;
Ombre Rainbow Cake Fail, Elizabeth Sheldon

Page 81: Freezing Rainbow, Desiree Morey

Page 82: Sorry Cake, Brianne Jansa and Julie
Caputo, lemonade33.wix.com/lemonadeoccasions

Page 83: It's the Icing on the Cat, Marlene Sowder

Page 84: Strawberry Break-Up Cake,
Courtney Evans

Page 85: Sad Bird Pizza, Michelle Berra,
berrasbeachhouse.wordpress.com

Page 86: Mini Caramel Apple Blacklist, Merry Luehr

Page 87: 14 Layers of Fail, Erin Henry

Page 89: I Would Not Eat Them Here or There,
Jennifer Keefe and Bethany Bash; I Would Not Eat
Them Anywhere, Wendy

Page 92: Cinnamon Fall-Apart Bread,
Fatimah Alidina

Page 93: Alien-Autopsy Garlic Bread,
Summer Donily

Page 94: Peppermint Profanity, Heather Jenkins

Page 95: Snowman Cookie Meltdown, Rylee Tlamka,
Sena Krula, and Laurel Todd, cashmerecacophony
.tumblr.com

Page 97: Cake a Mess, Christine Pace;
Fake It 'Til You Cupcake It, and Go Ahead,
Cupcake My Day, Ericka Skinner

Page 98: Anatomical Heart on Toast,
Elizabeth Gutierrez

Page 99: Craparons, Rebecca Barkley,
binspiredart.com

Page 101: A Delightful Mother's Day Treat,
Leah Wodoslawsky, whitefootblog.wordpress.com;
For Independence Day, Anna

Page 102: For Your Dog's Birthday, Toi Temple

Page 103: It's Beginning to Look a Lot Like
Christmas Cake Pops, Sue Hamilton; Like a Cake
Pop Virgin, Megan Chmarney and
Hany Aboul-Enein

Page 104: Shark Weak Cupcakes, Vicki Nelson

Martha Made It

Page 106: Martha's Schadenfreude, Summer Donily

Page 107: T-Shirt Necklace Transgression,
Megan Andersen Read

Page 109: Flattened Flower, Aunt Peaches,
auntpeaches.com; Mangled Moth, Tamara Baker;
Windblown Wad, Kelly Kazmierski

Page 110: So Easy a Kid Can Do It, Lewis Mann

Page 111: Seeing Through Martha's Translucent
Pumpkin Carving, Jessica O., Jwodesigns
.blogspot.com

Page 112: Rotten Egg Votives, Carissa Bonham,
creativegreenliving.com

Page 113: Dexter Blood Spattered Candles, Heidi
Kundin, happinessishomemade.com

Page 115: Martha's Waxed Heartbreakers, How
Rorschach-ing!, and Wax On . . . Wax So Off,
Amy McDonald, macorcheesy.com, and

Laura Putnam, findinghomeonline.com,
Page 116: Martha's Bath, Bombed, Mary Bordner Tanck

Kids. Crafts. Fails.
Page 118: Microwave Soap Sludge, mrspriss.com
Page 119: Baby Foot Forget It Print, Emily Carver
Page 120: How Does the Fox Fail, Katie Merrien
Page 121: Burp Bubbles, Stephanie Belcher
Page 122: Jimmy Hat in a Bottle, Linda Buha
Page 123: Fail or Fail Not, There Is No Try,
   Lynda Carroll
Page 124: Dad's Day Decoration Disaster,
   Tracy Grable
Page 125: Perler Bead Meltdown, Sarah White,
   sarahewhite.com
Page 126: Cupid's Anatomy Soap, Regina Cherill,
   chalkinmypocket.com
Page 127: Rubber Band Loom Chthulu, Claire
   Valentine, uglygossiper.blogspot.com
Page 129: Hula Hoop Weaving—It's a Trap!,
   Aimee Kreider, newlifetogether.tumblr.com;
   Es Un Sombrero!, SoShawna Gray,
   soshawna.blogspot.com
Page 130: It's a Tam!, Summer Donily; Crouching
   Weaving, Hidden Hula Hoop Hat, Casey O'Connell,
   anonyvox.com
Page 131: Leaky Hairy Sensory Bottle, Alyssa Wine,
   myclevernest.com
Page 133: X-Rated Way to Recycle Easter Eggs,
   Julie Sindora, buildsewreap.com

Page 134: Failship Bracelet, Allison Jeppson

A for Effort.
Page 136: What a Strong Sewing Machine You Have
   There, @katieiscrafty
Page 137: Bottles That Will Cut You,
   Jennifer Kraschnewski
Page 138: Bitter Crocheted Mouse, Laura Bainbridge
Page 139: There's No Spellcheck in Cross-Stitch,
   @designvigilante
Page 144: Call in the Bath Bomb Squad,
   Jennifer Stiles
Page 145: Screenprinting Splodge, Samantha
   Townsend, geekysweetheart.blogspot.com
Page 146: How's Your Scarf Organizer Hanging?,
   Christa Threlfall, brownsugartoast.com
Page 147: Mo'saic Mo'problems, Ana Hourahine,
   imadeitso.com
Page 148: Molten Mold, Johnnie Collier,
   savedbylovecreations.com
Page 149: Soft Yarn, Tangled, Allyson Torresan
Page 150: Step Away from the Sewing
   Machine, Becky
Page 151: The Dog Ate My CraftFail, Kristi Wagner,
   rengawk.blogspot.com
Page 152: Putting the Iron in Iron-On Transfer,
   Jen Lange, littlegreenscissors.com
Page 153: Cat in the Felted Hat, Amy Stomberg
Page 154: Desperate Measures, Lindsay Conner,
   craftfoxes.com

Page 155: Noose Felted Scarf, Jenn Dixon, ludicraft.com

Page 157: I'm Sorry, I Mustache You to Try Again, Philip Mecham, instagram.com/deaf258; Don't Bother Reading Directions, SugiAi, sugiai.blogspot.com

Page 158: My Love for You Is Fading, Randi Dukes, dukesandduchesses.com

Page 160: Put a Blob on It, Carissa Bonham, creativegreenliving.com

Acknowledgments

Thanks to my readers, who constantly document their failures and selflessly share them with me so I can share them with the world. Thanks to my husband, Jared Mann, who helped me figure out how to sort through our mountain of fails to find the best ones and offered a lot of other book-related advice, editing, and support. Thanks to my four sons, Lewis, Evander, Gideon, and August, who help me succeed and fail on a daily basis. Thanks to my mom, Kathy Varis, who helped me organize and contact all the contributors for the book (short sentence, super-long process). And thanks to my friend Summer Donily, who helped create a whole bunch of the original projects for this book and was available anytime for last-minute craft sessions and moral support. Thanks also to my friend and business partner, Amy Anderson, who is always available to listen and offer help and perspective. Much appreciation to my CraftFail.com contributing editor, Robyn Welling, who makes everything on the site funny. Special thanks to my funny buddies Aunt Peaches, Vivienne Wagner, Jessica Hill, and Carolina Moore, who helped me with emergency punchline writing. Thanks to my literary agent, Kate McKean, my editors, Megan Nicolay and Liz Davis, and the designer for this book, Becky Terhune.

I must also thank my team of craft-blogging friends, who are all such rock stars that they are able to "craft not-fail" on command and created and photographed many of the lovely, inspirational photos that appear in this book. Lastly, I have to give mad thanks to the bloggers, crafters, bakers, and designers who actually created the original inspiration projects and let us showcase them in this book—without you, we could never fail as hard!

About the Author

Heather Mann is a professional craft designer and blogger. She has appeared on *The Martha Stewart Show* and in *Reader's Digest* and *The New York Times*, and her projects have appeared on the cover of *Family Fun* magazine. Her other craft blog is DollarStoreCrafts.com.